The Poetry Book Society
Anthology 2

The Poetry Book Society Anthology 2

Edited by
Anne Stevenson

Hutchinson
London Sydney Auckland Johannesburg

© in this collection the Poetry Book Society 1991.
The copyright in individual poems remains with the authors.

All rights reserved

This edition first published in 1991 by Hutchinson
and by the Poetry Book Society Ltd,
21 Earls Court Square, London SW5

Random Century Group Ltd
20 Vauxhall Bridge Road, London SW1V 2SA

Random Century Australia (Pty) Ltd
20 Alfred Street, Milsons Point, Sydney,
NSW 2061, Australia

Random Century New Zealand Ltd
PO Box 40–086, Glenfield, Auckland 10,
New Zealand

Random Century South Africa (Pty) Ltd
PO Box 337, Bergvlei, 2012, South Africa

British Library Cataloguing-in-Publication Data
The Poetry Book Society anthology.
  I. Stevenson, Anne
  821.008

  ISBN 0-09-174859-3

Set in Times by ⚘ Tek Art Ltd, Addiscombe,
Croydon, Surrey
Printed and bound in Great Britain by Cox and
Wyman Ltd, Reading

Contents

Introduction

THE POETRY
BOOK SOCIETY

FOR EVERYONE WHO LOVES POETRY

AN EXCEPTIONAL POETRY BARGAIN

The Poetry Book Society, founded in 1953 by
T.S. Eliot and others to foster the love of poetry,
today continues to provide its members with an
informed choice of outstanding new books and
up-to-date poetry news.

Membership ensures that you receive the latest and
best contemporary poetry on a regular basis and at
considerable discount.

To find out more about this unique poetry service
contact:

> The Poetry Book Society,
> 21 Earl's Court Square,
> London, SW5 9DE
> (071 244-9792)

Introduction

I once knew a poet who arranged his library neither alphabetically by author nor by subject but according to how he calculated his books would get on with each other. Suppose the books were to come to life? Would they not feel happier in the company of sympathetic others? How furious they might be if they 'woke up', so to speak, neighbours to books they despised or to which they had nothing to say.

In arranging the poems of this anthology I have employed something like my friend's method. Doing away with the dictatorship of the alphabet, I have tried to group them with a view to complementary or, in some cases, contrasting themes and styles. A tentative logic, however, determined the three main sections.

Part I, significantly introduced by John Heath-Stubbs's 'Phoenix', brings together poems in which some sort of transmutation or poetic alchemy is achieved, either through the intensity of the poet's stare (G. F. Dutton's 'on passing'; Peter Redgrove's 'Cannon') or else by allowing the imagination convincingly to suspend disbelief (Penelope Shuttle's 'Angel', Gerard Woodward's 'Lighthouse'). When I first envisaged this anthology I suggested to a number of friends that they submit poems which in some respect considered the strange truths twentieth-century science has offered to belief. Among others Pauline Stainer, Isobel Thrilling, Peter Forbes and Gillian Clarke responded in different ways to my request. It seems to me that a quality of new-found astonishment – expressed also in Lee Harwood's 'Air Clamps', in Tom Rawling's 'At Totleigh Barton' and in Charles Tomlinson's 'The Clearance' – is a specifically contemporary ingredient of celebration.

Transmutation of some sort occurs in all poetry worthy of the name, so Parts II and III in no way represent a retreat from the alchemy of imagination. Part II is devoted to the work of poets from the North of England, a grouping intended to focus attention on the liveliness of the region and the diversity of its talents. Jon Silkin, William Scammell and Alistair Elliot are names well known throughout England, but few outside the North-East will have read the unusual work of William Martin, represented here by a sequence of 'nursery rhymes' that recall with affection the mining community of his native Silksworth, in Sunderland. Different in tone, but similarly tender, are the experimental 'Englynion' of Richard Caddel; and different still, two sharp-eyed lyrics by David Burnett and some empassioned but controlled revelations by younger poets, Peter Armstrong and C. B. McCully.

In Part III, a pervasive note of personal and political concern draws together work by Scottish, Welsh, Irish and English poets – among them Elizabeth Jennings, Norman MacCaig, Eavan Boland, Carol Rumens, Dannie Abse and Carol Ann Duffy. The one American is Richard Tillinghast, who is presently living in County Galway. As it was impossible to include work by all the poets I admire, I chose to represent as original a spectrum as possible, while preserving a mix of subjects and styles that would live happily together in one binding. The anthology could have been double the size. If some favourite poets have been omitted to make room for new names, I can only direct readers to the unexpectedly diverse work here, hoping that despite limitations of space and time the anthology will introduce readers to fresh work by old, young and unknown poets in rich and enjoyable profusion.

Anne Stevenson,
'Pwllymarch',
Llanbedr, N. Wales

Part I

JOHN HEATH-STUBBS

Phoenix

Over the hot Arabian sands,
  Or desert wastes of Tartary,
The phoenix flies upon the wind,
  And perches on the incense-tree:

The sole one of her kind, who's lived
  Three thousand and six hundred years,
While empires rose and fell, whose stories
  Were written out in blood and tears.

Upon that tree she builds her nest
  Of cassia, sandalwood, and cloves,
And rarer spices she has gathered
  In fragrant Yemen's fortunate groves.

Then she begins to start her only
  Sad and sweet mysterious singing,
Which sounds more loud and then more softly,
  Among the barren places ringing.

And those who hear that strange wild music
  Echoing around the lonely plain,
Find their senses all distracted –
  Their hearts can never rest again.

Then from the sky comes sudden thunder –
  Her nest's ignited by the flash;
The phoenix burns in ecstasy,
  To crumble into soft white ash.

And in the morning travellers come
   From north and south and east and west;
For they must sift the cooling embers
   Which once had been the phoenix-nest –

A Taoist sage from distant China,
   Next whom a Celtic druid stands,
An Aztec priest, a black-faced wizard
   From Africa's sun-burnished lands.

With mantras and with incantations
   They sift, till they discern a form –
A small, white, feeble, legless creature,
   Only just alive, a worm.

What chance is there of its survival,
   So insignificant and weak?
But soon it starts to sprout bright feathers,
   Bud wings, and talons, and a beak.

Then they rejoice, for in those ashes
   Another phoenix has been spawned;
Another phoenix-age begins
   And for mankind new hope has dawned.

TOM RAWLING

At Totleigh Barton

Is there tribal memory in the egg,
sextant in the eye, compass in the head,
astronomy in the blood of house-martins?
They trace the curve of the world,
each clan peeling away from the armada
when its particular landfall appears.
They are magnetised home by rocky tors,
the glinting Torridge, remembered oaks,
swoop down to this manor house in its hollow.
They are back where first they flew.

They twitter as they girdle their demesne,
air-skate their loops, trace figure-eights.
What mastery of surging climb, variety
of dips and swoops, flitter-flutter
stops to scoop up dancing midges
damsel flies, winged pismires!
They restore their strength, they feast,
but breeding is their business here,
see them curve to the loaf crust thatch,
cling to the shaded eaves to clag
mouthed mud in a crescent shape,
each day's course of pimpled nest wall
hardening, bellying to a giant acorn cup.

We too have gathered again beneath the thatch,
the house is live with our remembering footsteps,
we find a space for paper and typewriter,
build word upon word into swelling lines.

PENELOPE SHUTTLE

Angel

The angel is coming down,
white-hot, feet-first,
abseiling down the sky.

Wingspan? At least the width
of two young men lying head to head,
James and Gary, their bare feet
modestly defiant, pointing north,
south.

The angel has ten thousand smiles,
he is coming down
smooth as a sucking of thumbs,

he is coming down on a dangle of breath,
in blazing bloodsilk robes.
See the size and dignity of his great toes!

He comes down in a steam of feathers,
a dander of plumes,
healthy as a spa,
air crackling round him.

Yes, he comes down
douce and sure-winged,
shouting sweetly through the smoke,
'J'arrive!'

Hovering on fiery foppish wings,
he gazes down at me
with crane-neck delicacy.

I turn my head from his furnace,
his drastic beauty . . .
he is overcoming me.

On my crouched back his breath's
a solid scorching fleece.
In my hidden eyes, the peep of him hurts.

He waits,
he will not wait long.

Flames flicker along my sleeve
of reverence as I thrust my hand
into the kiln of the seraph.

Howling, I shoulder my pain,
and tug out one feather,
tall as my daughter.

When I look up,
he's gone on headlong wings,
in a billow of smoulders,
sparks wheeling, molten heels

slouching the side wind. 'Adieu!'

Goodbye, I wave,
my arm spangled with blisters
that heal as I stare at the empty sky.

And the feather?
        Is made of gold.
Vane and rachis, calamus
and down. For gold like an angel
joyeth in the fire.

ROBERT WELLS

The Valley

The barrier through which the body has to fight
Is the body, yours and the world's. Time and again

It emerges beyond itself, transfigured, lightened,
Yet at a loss; as when, climbing past a ridge,

You come out above the head of a trackless valley
– Yours to gaze over, pleasant in the morning sun –

And, caught in the promise of its light and shadow,
Stand with it at your feet but do not go down there.

At the Hill-Station

A room at the hill-station, fireless, bare.
No view. The hills are lost in mist-clogged air.

Plenty of space, though, to walk up and down
Thinking of unfilled spaces of my own.

GILLIAN CLARKE

Hölderlin

for Paul Hoffmann

The river remembers,
then crumples in a frown of loss:
a garden of children and laundry at the brink,
the white face of a man shut in the mind's tall tower.

In the October garden, where the carpenter's children
played between the high wall and the water,
apples fall, and fire-tongues of cherry
crackle in the grass for us to shuffle.

The great willow that the poet knew,
only half itself since the hurricane,
kneels into a current that's deeper
and more powerful than it seems.

Upstairs, in his white, three-windowed hemisphere,
where for forty years they cared for him, light
shivers on the ceiling, bird-shadows touch and go,
things that were clear break up and flow away:

his poems on the wall,
quick freehand in the visitors' book,
a jar of flowers on bare boards,
a drift of red leaves on three windowsills.

So small, his bed must have been here,
his table there for the light, and the door
where the carpenter's daughter listened for his rages
and brought him bread, meat, a bowl of milk.

The swan turns on her own reflection. Silence
is her image. Currents pull. The willow
trawls its shadow, searching for something
in the broken face of water.

The river remembers everything, its long muscle
bearing the weight of rain a month ago,
the touch of waterbirds miles upstream,
the heavy step of a waterfall in its deep subconscious,

and the white, raging pages
that once beat their foreheads
on its scattering surface
before drowning.

Note
Friedrich Hölderlin (1770–1843) was insane from 1802. In his
madness he lived in a tower above a carpenter's family, who
cared for him until he died. First the father, then the daughter
took him under their care.

DAVID CONSTANTINE

The Vicar's Firework Show

Because he wanted St Paul's, full,
And a singing of praises to raise the roof
And got Duxford with Penton Mewsey
And a bare quorum to observe his puffs of breath

He thanks God for gunpowder. All Souls,
The tongues of his flock of dead ignite again
And whisper visibly. He climbs the hill outside
To pull a multitude, like Wesley

Packed to the mouth with speech, he draws a town
Of people roaring into the dark
And does what it is his call of work to do:
He gets them to look up: at the lifted word

Spilled on the sky. When that night
He offers the finished work of his hands
His year of peaceably fiddling with saltpetre
And all his secret inventions go up from the ground

With a thump and arriving rapidly
Out of a pinpoint open and hold
Wide open falling their pent-up souls
And the people respond with numerous similes

They call to one another what it is like
And repeat the brilliant insights of their children
So multiplying his illuminations
And a congregation of innocents is looking up

Earth seems an enviable place, a small
Warmth in the universe, and God's
Face feels for it like a blind man's. I name
That vicar the hope of those who join

And their hearts still hunger. I wish him
Snow for Christmas, deep snow, a hush
Over everything, a cessation, whiteness,
The town dumbfounded, and one sprig of flame.

CHRISTOPHER REID

From Information Received

In the small crowd
   gathered to watch
the mountebank's scandalous
   last performance
there were, I understand,
   two people –
a man and a woman –
   whose faith in him,
far from being shattered,
   was roundly confirmed.

Detaching themselves
   from the crowd's sullen
and self-righteous rhubarb
   of disappointment,
they left that dusty
   place and took
to the highways and byways,
   there to proclaim
the 'good news',
   as they insist on describing it.

For, in their opinion,
   a miracle did happen:
the fellow did fly,
   just as he had said he would,
rapturously rocketing
   to some point in the sky
of incalculable altitude,
   before seeming
to change his plans
   and plunging back earthwards.

To illustrate
   their abstruse message,
they have some bit
   of business with a stone –
or any handy object –
   which they toss in the air,
telling you to fix
   your mind on the moment
when it stops and allows
   itself to fall.

I don't believe
   we need fear this cult,
one among so many,
   and lacking as it does
either clear moral precepts
   or potent symbolism –
some ingenious gimmick
   like, say, the cross.
But the usual precautions
   might still be in order.

LEE HARWOOD

Air Clamps

The building is very large that you see
across the fields, dear reader,
can you see, above the green the white
of its walls and red of the tiles?

Standing amongst all this green
whether to sigh in admiration of a vague harmony
or to rage at this fixity? Huh?

A gardener or a visitor might be moving
in the distance towards or away from that building;
or simply standing still musing or about to
step off into some irresolute, even meaningless, action.

I step off into the bushes, the hillsides of long grasses,
the sunken path now overgrown and decorated with orchids,
to emerge later, somewhat sweaty, but pleasantly glowing.

The Stuff is fixed in its grip on us
but we slip loose some times and decay
gradually eats at the structures, we hope.

In twenty years' time the white may be grey,
or still a dazzling white, but the house now
turned into a hotel for conferences and gourmet weekends.
The estate divided, the landscape farmed,
or built on even, though unlikely in this place.

A frazzled reader shoves old postcards, photos,
jigsaw puzzles into a remote drawer
wanting only to get up and out the door
into the street air, but then suddenly
dawns the weirdly controlled clamps rotating
in the sky by unseen hands.

G.F. DUTTON

on passing

no it is not repeat
repeat, it is once
only and enough;

these juniper berries bunched,
sun-bosomed through the frost-
needles in the bright

snow-light, meet their first
chance to last next
spring, and no more;

rounded-off tough
sky-blue bloomed, their green
one-year-behind

successors crowding about them.
it is enough
to have seen a stiff

laden juniper branch,
pausing as you are
passing, just now once

out of the snow and never,
coming back how often,
to see it this way again.

the prize the primacy of it
the instantaneous thousand
cold needles ever

afire and berries
thrusting their one spring
aware out of the cluster.

docken

and there is a docken
that each year
grows hugely in a corner
of the car park, that has seen

three factories take on this site
and has outlived
all three, survived to be
just now Japanese, it is

a great favourite,
old Willie Stout
the gardener does not dare
spray it or howk it out.

a tall docken
with a long stem
that rises from
the secret to the sun.

ANNE RIDLER

Snakeshead Fritillaries

Some seedlings shoulder the earth away
Like Milton's lion plunging to get free,
Demanding notice. Delicate rare fritillary,
You enter creeping, like the snake
You're named for, and lay your ear to the ground.
The soundless signal comes, to arch the neck,
Losing the trampled look,
Follow the code for colour, whether
White or freckled with purple and pale –
A chequered dice-box, tilted over the soil,
The yellow dice held at the base.

14

When light slants before the sunset, this is
The proper time to watch fritillaries.
They entered creeping; you go on your knees,
The flowers level with your eyes,
And catch the dapple of sunlight through the petals.

JAMES BERRY

Starapple Time Starapple Trees

All around flame-trees blaze
a red acreage of domed tops.
Mouths are sweet stained.

Everybody eats the starapple.
Brown or purple or white
succulent ready flesh exposes
hidden star to open faces
of starapple time.

Enticing to be opened in
group-loving starapple time
lips luring round fruits grew
between limbs, growing
shadowed to readiness
near big boat cotton-tree erect,
washed by the sun's burning.

And apple-honey squeezed and sucked –
all else gone suspended –
who won't make joy noises
under canopy of coppery silk
bridal in sunlight? Even
a woodpecker, in its dipping
flight, screams with laughter.

PETER SCUPHAM

Riches Heures

Seeing, but mostly through, past blue light
Patching at star-peep up against the window
Lighter than branches blotted on free evenings,
The unturned leaves of trees heading for nightfall,
You look for something that might be a token.
When all they said was 'Seeing is believing',
What then was seeing but a loose lantern
Swung in the dark, blindly-starred, and waiting
For light to clean its gates of horn and ivory,
Jump through little hoops cut in blue paper –
Blue as those windows fronting on the choir-stalls,
Grey perpendiculars infilled by stars
Hung over dark saints dressed in blood and emerald?
How fierce their judgement when the sun comes out,
Suspended by the press of makeshift clouds.
A Saint should have stars shaken over him –
A pepper-pot of light for each cold nimbus.
Chained at my wrist, a moon-face watch recycles
A simple blue, a splutter of gold ink
As childish, jostled out of constellation,
As Heaven daubed about a wizard's cloak.
Oh, Calendar pages, where the so rich hours
Keep their unwinking station for the grass,
And cloaks, betrothed to gold and silences,
Lie weightless to the flesh as cut-stone towers
Lie weightless to the hill, your pale, limp faces
Are not inclined to hear our conversation.
For you, the sky-beasts, penned in arcs of azure,
Stand level-headed among equal stars
Dancing a little, grown fey and tremulous
As coins which have learned to live in water,
Clusters of spent wishes wished by some
Too young or old for seeing and believing.
You need a kind of sun to see the stars by . . .

A Box of Letters

This is the chapter where the treasure-seekers,
Flinging the lid back, rinse their hands in gold,
Listen to gulls – a pale sky scrawled with voices.
Perhaps, like music, gulls have things to say
About snapped wish-bones and the sandy bay,
This cave's rubbed windows, attic salt, and cold.

But no; the dropped scraps of their conversations
Run out into the bladderwrack and foam.
The sea-chest disappoints with cling-film faces
And little creepings underneath the skin,
With brittle ribbons and a black-head pin,
As if blind-dates and dust could make a home

To babble volumes in, to plead, confess
How much they missed each other, what they read
In faces that were not yet photographs.
Their news, as common as the common cold,
As flowers, as Christmases, as getting old,
Grows rare and nervous just by being dead,

An itch of wrinkled fingers whispering:
'We mapped the land, charted the deep-sea swell,
And time and tide were in our reckoning.
Not now; not you. See how these kisses mark
Heart-burials.' In equinox and dark
The shaken house keens like a giant shell.

PETER REDGROVE

Safely to Truro and Back Again

A shell like the entrance to a cave,
Like the entrance to a humming mine made of water;

The season letting go of its leaves
In a profound relaxation of the whole resort;

Above, schools of parachutists
Sky-diving through the summer-blue abyss;

Below, the autumn buddleia is burying
The September graves sky-blue;

In the Art School the one good teacher
Employs his students as if they were his own brushes

Who paint the powers and principalities
Far underground that exert their influences and wishes;

There is a fiery gem of petrol
Pounding in the base-metal setting of my motor-car engine:

Precious liquid stone alchemised
From aeons of trees; it takes me

Safely from Falmouth to Truro and back again.

Cannon

The evening wind of a shady beach blows
Sharply across the muzzle of a shipwrecked cannon;
It has lain here decades, black in the sands,

Aimed at the stars, battle-spent.
The sand scours the iron all day,
And all night long, spinning round and round

The belly of the night-hued iron
As stars spin in the round black heaven
With their faint ringing constantly

Of prism chasing prism over sable iron.

PAULINE STAINER

Prism in a White Room
In memory of Jacqueline du Pré

i
For you I would take out
between dark and dark
the prism in a white room

the oblique kindling
from buried Pharaohs,
a crystal inserted to lighten the face

Turner's late white canvases
of nothing, and very like
horizon lost in absolute calm

the arctic hare's tibia
notched like a gnomon
into calendar of the moon

trace-element from silver-point,
a thin silver stylus
for the end of time.

ii

Anguish not gravity
flaws the crystal –
morphine frozen in the syringe

at the sheer threshold
of avalanche –
white steppe foxes

stunned by
blunt arrowheads of bone,
their pelts undamaged.

iii

Mystery is mute;
the cores of ancient snow
burn and atomise;

with heavy dust-like bloom
the quince hang golden
into the frost.

PETER FORBES

The Glassblower

To see not heaven but the glass in sand!
I raise my bubble bowls against the air
and see a flaw emerge, a breathy comma –
such imperfections to a child meant home:
'Velacre Cottage' in wobbly type
ripples through my eyes like Edwardian heat-haze;
the windows of the world are sliding downwards,
a river flowing like a glacier's creep.

And I'm sad when I see a window broken,
the fragments crazed around a cosmic hurt;
I know my twin, my rude glass-hurler,
he lives in me still: when a bubble bursts
I'd fling it down for the joy of breaking –
that clotted space in a million shards!

The cruelty of glass, its improvised tortures,
the beerglass slicing through a rugose cheek –
could my crystal chalice be so abused?
Perish such thoughts in the cusp of fire
where sand and soda fuse into pearls . . .

My wife is a yeasty, pulsing ferment,
a moony queen of the enzyme vats –
monthly her follicles tickle into bloom –
but my soul is a building furnished with windows,
like Hardwick Hall in its fireworks glow:
I stare till my eyes fear vitrifaction,
their quivering humours shocked into quartz:
a nebula trapped in a green glass marble,
a blood-flecked ovum light years old.

ALISON BRACKENBURY

On Wistley Hill

Sheep, have you found a shoe?
                                    They were not here
when we rode, boisterous, through afternoon.
They lift their bony faces, strangely white
on the long back of the hill. The reservoir
floats bluer than the sky. A Roman snailshell
gleams white beside the track. The pale farmhouse,
despite the signs for B & B, shines empty.
Grey ponies in the ridge-fields stand unfed.

I wait for the white moon, swollen and eager,
and meanwhile, I trudge back, to the beechwood
where we slithered over banks. The Thames starts here,
that proud, foul river, in a slime of root.
Oh, day drops and curved twigs mock in their hardness,
my fingers probe the hoofholes, nothing's there,
not owl or badger or the ghostly sheep.

So much, I think, has drowned beneath the wood,
lovers' hairpins, farmers' iron, pigs' bones.
Frightened of rape or loss, I almost run
whistling old tunes, beneath the lightless sky.
How short spring's days are, despite all we do.
Where have the sheep gone? Who will find my shoe?

GERARD WOODWARD

Lighthouse

That night the house
Troubled the householder's sleep
And became a kind of Wolf Rock.

What was the loft was
Where the precious light burned,
And the slates of a tough

Roof turned transparent
And prismatic, focusing
That warm, floating lantern's glow.

An ordinary suburbia
Changed to black, frightening sea
And everything was round;

Rooms, windows, eyes
As he found his stairs
Went down further

Than there were before floors.
His front door seemed
At the base of a well

As he turned the starfish
Handle and stepped
Into the kelp and shells

Of a one-time front garden
And saw the proof, his house
A tower striped like crockery

Occulting its name
Across hostile brine,
Occurring in the Admiralty

Lists of Lights,
Brother to Bishop Rock,
Friend of Eddystone, ancient

As Pharos, he felt proud,
He saw the ships lit up and safe,
He heard the living captains hailing.

DEWI STEPHEN JONES

The Balance

The colour of blood and a charge
in the steep eye,
it trembles above an acre of wheat,
then off and away
to where the sky meets memory;
searching – searching,
returning
to hover above grasses
with summer pollen on its talon.

In Weakness . . .

In weakness, as cumbersome as
the resurrection of a creature from its winter sleep,
slowly, with the palm of my hand, I make
a window in the steamed-up pane

and O – the shape of it –
the same bright wonder
as the mouth which took the very first swig
of winter's chill.

Note
Translated from the Welsh by the poet.

ISOBEL THRILLING

Blue

Dusk
shakes out its velvets,
looses stars.

The physics of blue
eludes me,
arching its short wave-length
to colour sky.

Is it a chemical reaction,
rods, cones in the head,
a wave, a particle?
The rim of space is blue
but not to a bee.

It's a tactile shade,
has power
to give a dusting to skin,
settles softly.

Blue
is the colour of genies,
midnight, distant mountains,
the ignition
of certain gases.
It can cool
to Arctic depths;
the newest, hottest suns
burn blue.

No hue
can be more fragile holding
winter twigs in china.

The tenderest
shade in the spectrum,
the colour of death
is blue.

SYLVIA KANTARIS

Lost Property

I'm on this train, you see, somewhere abroad,
heading north or south perhaps. Outside it's dark.
You panic when you've lost all your effects
including passport and visas, and forget
what your name was. I study my reflection
in the glass. Is it mine or someone else's
or a ghost? And then this man in uniform
demands some document to prove that I exist?
No use protesting when it's obvious I don't
since the evidence has vanished with my face.
When he looks, he can only see himself
and says who are you kidding when I point it out.

What happens next? I have forgotten everything
except a grey, furled umbrella. Would *that* pass?
'Lost Property' the stickers indicated
in a lot of languages I couldn't read.
You don't ask questions when you're dispossessed.
So here I am, then, clinging on like death
to somebody's umbrella, but I lose my grasp.
Trains don't normally have floorboards, I thought,
as the sad old thing went down between two planks.
Funny how you kid yourself you'll 'suddenly wake up'
travelling light in a fluorescent anorak,
crossing every border on the map without a permit.

CHARLES TOMLINSON

The Clearance

They have fired the brush in the half-felled wood:
   Extinguishing piles still smoke on, blue;
Beacons of briars and ivy blazing through,
   Crest the detritus. A glitter
And, suddenly red, a starburst breaks
   As the wind takes hold, and the burnings
And the glows go spreading uphill
   Into the wood-heart. The cut logs
Tell, in their greenness, of how wet
   The wood was, that now lets in
The hilltop horizon and the sky.
   Fresh plantings will branch out there,
Feel the embrace of entering air –
   Spaced to receive our climbing glance
That can survey all of the falling stream
   Woodland had hidden away, a white
Rope the water lets down
   Sounding closer and closer against the ear,
A keen, clear flight to the feet of whoever is standing here.

On a Passage from Hardy's *Life*

You were a poet who put on the manners of ghosts,
Thinking of life not as passing away but past,
Taking the ghost view of surrounding things,
A spectre who, making his calls in the mornings,
Found satisfaction in his lack of solidity
Before he had entered into true non-entity.
Even in paradise, what you would wish for,
Would be to lie out in the changing weathers here,
And feel them flush through the earth and through you,
Side by side with those you had known, who never quite
                              knew you,
Dreaming a limbo away of loam, of bone,
One Stygian current buoying up gravestone on gravestone.

Part II

JON SILKIN

Beings

Two minute flies, beings back to back
join with a long black particle.

One of them bigger, its wings raised, holds
both in tension, erect

held perfect connection
for hours, with legs firm over paper

sufficient for them. Their long completion
on white stirs

a single memory, of how
I, too, being with you and by Him

imagined, yet imagining, left
to be, in dire amazed

double shared control
were, on the eiderdown, a feathery creation

of us, palm to palm,
the wings flighted as with joy.

Aching to Survive

We fly people, with a fly's hand
clasp fly-like fear, bitter lungs

professing care. So, do you mean
kindness, I asked this fly? Scratched me,

the wings unbroken, frenzied
as a butterfly's, a lashing whiteness

from the basking chrysalid, of two flies
tangled, in the sly mentality of lives,

of rasping bosoms that ache to survive.

The frail flesh simulates a caress.
It is turquoise and worry. A slither

of snake-forms in the wings, veins of dirt
whose lashing stills itself. We preen,

for dirt, too, wants its looks. Sucking creatures that fuzz
into the sun, that anxious silent

fortress of light, the good trespass
on a whole fly.

The sad might of minute
life, the tenacious hyphens

that join us in love, in all rearing storms.
So we march to die of each other,

the smell of abomination in combat,
tumultuous vulnerable wings.

DAVID SCOTT

Lambing

This sudden birth: a few seconds
of unexplained dragging, crook
flung down, a wrestling into submission.
He dragged out the slimed reason for the struggle,
wiped its eyes, freed life's fingertip passage.
As if that was not enough, manhandling
to keep the sheep's sniff and lick
only on this limp stranger, he held
his own breath until it took, then rose
sure the invisible elastic between sheep
and lamb would stretch from the railings
to the tarn's edge. He picked up his crook.
We picked up our walk.

WILLIAM SCAMMELL

Green Over Blue

The village by the sea
was deadly boring to a boy
for waves struck at the pier
only because the pier was there
and great liners sailed
off to encounter the world

leaving their agitated wash
fraying the shallows of the beach
where seagulls muscled in
on a dead salmon
bruised quiet as mud, then
clapped off screeching

like baptists. The second coming
if there was to be one
took the form of wave or leaf
or swimmable New Forest
streams, a fallen log across
its clear and meditative face.

What can be done with a tree
but climb it? And a rusty yew
that won't turn into Robin's bow
or bend across a naked knee,
with hazel arrows, hard to fledge,
cut green and perfect from the hedge?

Old Fraser had barbed-wire
tweeds, club tie, an arctic glare
for eyes, a short black cane
that barked even the hardest palm.
You weren't to shout. On Poppy Day
he wore his medals. Penelope

Young, the robin of our class,
God gave to smile at me at last.
She offered up her face. I bit
a portion from her apple cheek
and chewed it half a lifetime, till
I'm grown around that secret smile –

the russet and the leaf that hides
its growing. Still the waves
lap at me. If not the sea it was
the Cotswolds, or the northern fells,
for cities rose and fell in a flash
and my flesh was somehow grass

imprinted with that village hue:
in either case, green over blue
chasing each other, as the weight
of tides broke on the Isle of Wight
or shadows of low jets were thrown
like tomahawks across Old Man.

Love in a mist, love's origin
in sudden hapless parenting –
what grey roof or pavement could
assuage a heart, as well as mud?
I've circled all the globe, I've
known the rich, and grown a slave,

pitched my tent in New York's glare,
been to Japan, been everywhere
that offered spells to educate
a stubborn mind, a backward heart
lost now to all but that low roar
in wind, the sea upon the shore.

PETER BENNET

Winter Hills

Beyond the lichened balustrade, I saw
my parents on a shelving lawn,
one Saturday, the start of Summer.

Though men cut timber in the higher woods,
and children squawked from shrubberies,
a twang of insects dulled each sound.

He wore his khaki, she the soft print dress
that's famous in the photographs –
they glanced towards me joyfully, and smiled.

But I am not the one that they remembered,
and only I can see the birches bend
across the slope where they embraced each other,

and how the winter hills close round.

RICHARD CADDEL

Nine Englynion
The Ash Tree That Bears Apples

Nennius

Glad it was so: not pushing for reasons
     or easy answers, just
    happy to walk down the path

with winter sun in our eyes and ears cold
     from wind, pushing branches
    from faces; no need for words.

Late afternoon, the world turning to night
     its last light weakening
    low in branches: bitter fruit

Tenebrosa Sicut Nox

Days dark as night, can't work, can't sleep tonight,
  my glass and book empty;
  eyes dim, my mind on small things.

Light low, I sit up in the gloom tonight,
  witless, I write little,
  pale thoughts weighing my blind brain.

House quiet, white frost, a sinking peace: tonight
  my mind is in the east
  in set dark: my fears grip tight

The Coat

Where to look for it? Frail light, far at sea,
  a land frost set as salt
  wind's temper fretting our steps.

Going alone: breathing hard on the cold
  to break it, fear like a
  starbeam on the path, dark faith.

Finally casting it off. Song lifting
  and going on alone
  in frost, the same and yet changed

Note
*Purists may object – justifiably – that I have been too free with
this Welsh verse form. I can only stress that no disrespect to
the originals is intended. Englynion milwr from the book of
Llywarch Hen, together with the shorter of the two Juvencus
englynion, have been very much in my mind when writing
these.*

Richard Caddel

WILLIAM MARTIN

Bairnseed

*These streets were within the wall of the original mining
village of Silksworth*

1 Aline Lord Robert
  Quarry Maria Hill

  Remember the evictions there
  In eighteen-ninety-two

  Remember the candymen
  Slipping the greasy stairs

  Remember the cayenne-pepper
  As they moved their bits o' things

2 Londonderry Silksworth-Terrace
  Split by the school

  Girls in the west black yard
  Eastern side lads bool

  On the mountain stands a lady
  Skip the turning rope you two

  Mountykitty one
  Leap one two three
  Mountykitty mountykitty
  Fall off me

3 Edward Stewart Frances
  Doctor Hopper's bones

  Run down the black path
  Keep ahead of stones

  Baked bread on window-sills
  Flat-cake fadge and loaf

  A whole street of baking days
  Draws bairns by the nose

4 Castlereagh Tunstall
   Wynyard William John

   West end and east end
   All within the wall

   Fish shop and cropper
   Beasts to their fall

   Father brings us chocolate
   From the I.O.G.T. Hall

5 Seaham West Henry
   Charles North Mary George

   Mother's chapel my chapel
   Say my 'piece' rehearsed

   Grandmother Mary
   And grandmother Jane

   Big Meeting banners
   Coming up the lane

Note
I.O.G.T.: Independent Order of Good Templars.

DAVID BURNETT

The Names of God

Ramón, Miguel, Juanita.
These, too, are the names of God.
How many names God has!
And He remembers them each day.
He thinks about each,
The splendour each of them bears,
Saying the words over and over,
Ramón, Miguel, Juanita.
It is only we forget our selves.

East London

In the one, endless street
A blank, featureless lane,
Brick, and no name to it, –
Little to me, and nothing
Almost except from the train
A gable end and a swing
(How one notices such things!)
And a window at the eaves, a slit
And no more, but the pane
Ablaze, and street after street
All light and every meaning,
The world at one and plain.

C.B. McCULLY

Brun Clough

Beyond his head
was the clear air,
and the moor's edge
made him look so much the less massive –
we saw only a humped sack, a blue anorak,
perhaps a sleeping weight where light spread

dangerously. It seemed there was no death there.
But coming closer then, before the sirens,
you could see he'd been hurt, the mottled meat
on his old cheek,
the purple stain
under his hair.

Then he was cold,
and hard to turn.
His pale eyes shrank
as blood sunk on its weight; and there was nothing to know –
only the sprinting of ambulance; keeping off dogs;
the silence after someone being told.

Perhaps the last thing you hear when you're dead
is the glittering of lark and throstle
fastening all April to the sky
on the moor's edge,
in the clear air
beyond your head.

Rain

You should have seen the rain.
The hill was Lear's bald head left to the falling storm
and darkness shocked itself, in a springing wave buried the
road,
the valley and the singing stones, and each house
went out completely, like a switched-off brain;
you should have seen the rain –
stotting down so hard it melted hair and washed away
fences, pylons, all landmarks; fused lights; broke roofs;
and stopped the diesels underground in floods
(the water rising, commuting hands clawing each pane);
but you should have seen the rain
that night, last night, the very last – the howling stacks,
the gutters full, and all the fish swept smoothly out to sea
and back again, dispersed among the sky-reflecting fields,
fields of white noise, the static hiss of rain on rain,
the rain you should have seen,
the broken storm, endless, the storm with strength
to hurt itself, and me, with strength to erase my name
and yours, whether we lay apart listening to the rain
or in each other's arms and felt the rain,
imagining the dark rain walking towards us, the bane
stored up for us from the beginning of might-have-been.
You should have seen, it was almost marvellous,
you should have seen the rain which cancelled us.

MATT SIMPSON

Helvellyn

You say we should go back there,
where, hand catching hand, we left
imprints, hobnails scuffing rock,
scree scuttering a thousand feet;

and see the place as history, as more
than somewhere wind and cloud
make wordless bargains; where we climbed
teetering vertebrae of Striding Edge

that kept dropping back in their own space;
watched the graphite tarn contract,
pucker, wince below; piled ourselves in stones
upon the summit cairn; then hobbled down

the rainy western side to Wythburn chapel
and the road – Helvellyn, an obdurate past
separating and coupling us,
whalebacked behind us and above.

PETER ARMSTRONG

To a Child Born at Woodstock

When your mother heaved you into light
somewhere among the mud and the stoned
the fences had already kissed the ground,
the highways were jammed.
Across more than an ocean the B52s
went in echelon: it was between the blues
that Hendrix played and the children napalmed
you came to light.

Twenty years since Yasker's farm housed
its piece of heaven and disaster zone
I have come across you: one announcement on
the p.a.; a few drawled words
and then the backwash of the crowd's
easy roar; and cut to some cop dazed
with the numbers and the peace, a couple
making love in the fields without scruple.

It was an amazed eye you opened
on the ashes of Prague's mythic spring, Paris
tear-gassed, Chicago blitzed;
and rising like some giant Blake dreamed
the head of LBJ, sad eyes steel-rimmed
above the wrack, the great wizened
face a down-market Texan Ares
surveying the ant-swarm of its id.

What could you hope to make of it, icon
born into the shower of split light
brought down with the gems and
beatific faces your parents unpinned
from the shell of the sky? It
glanced across my growing between
confessions: a rumour of provinces
beyond fasts and penances;

now it is my city on the hill,
its light-conscienced populace moving
with a studied innocence: Israel
come from exile raising
a song of ascents: *I want to take you
higher* breezing the temperate night.
And for a moment it might,
a curl of hash-smoke brushing deepening blue

and you, turning your eye
to the woman's face
taking shape beside you. At the lip
of sleep, out of the white fields
your mind walks, the one gaze
that outlasts terms of office builds
its world. Ages rise and let slip
their dubious hold. Across an unnoticed sky

the squadrons metamorphose peaceably.

EVANGELINE PATERSON

Song for an Innocent

Born with such gentleness as you,
with such a pure and trusting face,
how could I tell you what I knew?
This world is not your kind of place.

Your candid look, your artless grace
fit you for somewhere else than here.
This world is not your kind of place.
I wish it were. I wish it were.

Outsider

The idiot boy in the outfield
gallops, eye on the ball.
Eye on the fly-half's leap,
he leaps too. When the full-back
flings his length in the mud
he too, on the tussocky verges,
acts out despair. He dodges,
weaves, feints, follows
the action in slow motion,
pounds the length of the field
again, again

and goes home unbruised, unmuddied.
When all the players are bedded
and snoring like trombones, he, wakeful, watches
an elliptical moon eluding him in the sky.

ALISTAIR ELLIOT

Remains of Mining in the Upper Peninsula, Michigan

This was the edge of history,
the lip of the wave that licks at chaos;
and these are the first tools,
these houses glistening with the oils
of human skin, and smelling of old clothes,
genuine nineteenth-century
smoke and the powder of ancient pastry.

This raw log box
holds still, in the freshness of the forest,
the essences of miners.
At first I think the stale patina's
the taste of bachelors, the shiny crust
baked on a man by work;
but they were clean men, Finns, with a sauna by the creek.

Besides, this is the scent
of grandma's house, a reek of home
that has not chimneyed up my nose
for fifty years: I recognise,
thousands of miles away, the Model Farm,
and am no longer entirely present,
odour discrediting every other sense.

This puzzling family smell
is what my new nephew caught
when I first lifted him:
under the hinge of my arm
blew his mother's microclimate,
her musty rain-forest, with one small
difference, one less flower and one new animal.

But how do my relatives enter this?
I suddenly realise
my widening modern nostrils
are following the trail,
the cold track, of my own race:
what the shocked Indians greeted with courtesies,
the stink of white men in the wilderness.

Part III

ELIZABETH JENNINGS

Verb

Listen, the acute verb
  is linking subject and object,
hear the links fall in place
  and the sturdy padlock click.

A verb is power in all speech,
  rings through prose and verse,
it brings to birth. Can't you hear
  the first cry of awareness?

'I go', 'I forget', 'I exist'
  by language only and always.
Blood cannot beat in a void
  and the potent, fiery tongue

offers the gift of language,
  blesses our lips and throats.
'I love you' vows and connects
  and moves in a climate of tensions.

The Smell of Chrysanthemums

The chestnut leaves are toasted. Conkers spill
Upon the pavements. Gold is vying with
Yellow, ochre, brown. There is a feel
Of dyings and departures. Smoky breath
  Rises and I know how Winter comes
  When I can smell the rich chrysanthemums.

It is so poignant and it makes me mourn
For what? The going year? The sun's eclipse?
All these and more. I see the dead leaves burn
And everywhere the Summer lies in heaps.
  I close my eyes and feel how Winter comes
  With acrid incense of chrysanthemums.

I shall not go to school again and yet
There's an old sadness that disturbs me most.
The nights come early but each bold sunset
Tells me that Autumn soon will be a ghost,
  But I know best how Winter always comes
  In the wide scent of strong chrysanthemums.

NORMAN MacCAIG

So Many Worlds

I stand for a few minutes
at the mouth of Hell's Glen.
Not because I think there are devils in it
and generations of the dead
being tortured for the sins they can't forget.

Behind me the loch I know so well
smiles in the sun and laughs along its shores.
It's part of my Paradise –
and not a saint in it
nor harps twangling
their endless tunes.

Always between two worlds,
Hell's Glen and Paradise –
without counting those inside me
where the moon brushes its way
through groves of birch trees
and ice floes ignore those silent dancers
in the midnight sky
and cities that have died
send their ghosts
into the streets of Edinburgh
and the words she spoke changed my darkness
to a summer morning, friendly as a fireside.

A Sort of Thanks

My memory's getting slipshod.

Yet it still suddenly reveals
the mile-long bank of primroses
by Loch Sal, last Spring. Or it produces
from nowhere the acrobatic pair of ravens
I saw near Drumbeg so many years ago.

Like a lost ship that reaches harbour in a fog
it unloads cargoes from hundreds of ports –
bales of words, bundles of people,
a treasure chest of music – lamps
better than Aladdin's.

Memory, I've not destroyed you yet
and never will –
for who ever heard of a bird
wrecking its own nest?
Who ever heard of a bird
plucking out its own flight feathers?

EAVAN BOLAND

Names

About holiday rooms there can be
a solid feel at first. Then, as you go upstairs,
the air gets
a dry rustle of excitement

the way a new dress comes out of tissue paper,
up and out of it, and
the girl watching this thinks:
Where will I wear it? Who will kiss me in it?

Peter
was the name on the cot.
The cot was made of the carefully-bought
scarcities of the nineteen-forties: Oak.
Tersely planed and varnished.
Cast-steel hinges.

I stood where the roof sloped into paper roses –
half a world away from where I lived –
in a room where a child once went to sleep,
looking at blue, painted letters:

as he slept
someone had found for him
five pieces of the alphabet which said
the mauve petals of his eyelids as they closed out
the scalded hallway moonlight made of
the ocean at the end of his road.

Someone knew
the importance of giving him a name.

For years I have known how important it is
not to name
the coffins and the murdered in them,
the deaths in alleys and on doorsteps, happening
and happening ninety miles away from my home;

in case they rise out of their names
and turn to me and I recognize

the child who slept peacefully,
the girl who guessed at her future in
the dress as it came out of its box,
falling free in kick pleats of silk.

What comfort is there then in knowing that

in a distant room
his sign is safe tonight,
and reposes its modest blues in darkness?

Or that outside his window
the name-eating elements – the salt wind, the rain –
must find
headstones to feed their hunger?

BERNARD O'DONOGHUE

The Weakness

It was the frosty early hours when finally
The cow's despairing groans rolled him from bed
And into his boots, hardly awake yet.
He called 'Dan! come on, Dan!
She's calving', and stumbled without his coat
Down the icy path to the haggard.

Castor and Pollux were fixed in line
Over his head but he didn't see them,
This night any more than another.
He crossed to the stall, past the corner
Of the fairy-fort he'd levelled last May.
But this that stopped him, like the mind's step

Backward: what was that, more insistent
Than the calf's birth-pangs? 'Hold on, Dan.
I think I'm having a weakness.
I never had a weakness, Dan, before.'
And down he slid, groping for the lapels
Of the shocked boy's twenty-year-old jacket.

PATRICIA BEER

Lacock Abbey

Fox-Talbot the photographer lived here.
It seems he was as numerate as God.
At any point on any lane he could
Say how many miles altogether

He had travelled since birth. Each stair
Of the house, each nun and speculator dead,
Clicked on the abacus inside his head.
Deity, poet and photographer

Count differently. God might see the world
As though it were a fountain in the light
Falling in sparrows, rising up in souls.

The poet turns a corner, sees gold curled
Around a lake in March and at first sight
Registers ten thousand daffodils.

GEORGE SZIRTES

A Doctor's Room

There was in his room an old X-ray machine,
part coffin and part phonebooth: strips of metal,
mahogany frame, leather. It was a grand house
and this the grandest room. A gentleman
might sit here waiting, whistling a little
before the heavy drapery of the curtain,
peering at pictures, or read a magazine
by the light of the great glass.

Inside the cubicle the darkness sat
patient as a patient till one drew
the flap aside and entered the capsule,
protected, naked, still decent,
and waited to be cut through
by the brilliant equipment
which could pinpoint organs bones and heart
with light as hard as a jewel.

From the Wreck of the Hope to the wreck
of reason in a glass. His pictures spoke
soft landscapes to a gentleness of carpets.
His painters were personal friends
who read books, knew the psychopathology of jokes
but told them just the same, inventing new ends
for old beginnings. When they fell sick
he treated them to the latest tablets,

analysed their love affairs and cancers,
had them in stitches as they once had him.
He was growing old. A young lady saw fit
to help him across the street. He thanked her
gallantly, admired her ankles which were slim
and tantalising as his wife's once were,
though she was blonde not dark. Light dancers
still flitted across his hungry wit.

Of course he knew what the cubicle wanted,
what it meant when she appeared in dreams.
He was no fool but a realist. A narrow space
did not go in for ambiguity, and yet
he clearly understood her schemes
to enslave him. It was something he could forget
for days at a time and then be suddenly shunted
into her arms, into her hushed grace.

He was becoming venerable, a sir to everyone.
That hard invisible light would break his bones
along with his heart and expose the frailty
of one who had prided himself on being useful.
The world of the maps was tired. He was full of groans
and found himself insufferably dull.
He would soon be seen through. The war was won.
His servant brought his boots in. Who was she?

TONY CURTIS

Taken for Pearls

In muddied waters the eyes of fishes
are taken for pearls.

As those two trout, little bigger than my hand then,
taken by spinner at Cresselly on an early

summer's day in the quiet afternoon
before the season's traffic. Only

a tractor in an unseen field
stitching the air like a canopy over it all.

And the taste of them pan-fried nose to tail
by my mother. The sweet flesh prised from

cages of the most skilfully carved bone.
I closed my eyes and she smiled for me.

MAURA DOOLEY

The Celestial Announcer

On the day that you hear
the station announcer
call out the towns and villages
of your life, as if she'd read
the very chapters of your soul,
that knowing way she has of saying *Halifax*,
the way she skirts around poor rainy *Manchester*,
and jumps to the conclusion now of *Luddenden*
– with its ghost of a station
and dream of Branwell drunk under the stars –
and all the big and little places
you have ever been, would like to go,
chanted, charted;
well, then you realise it's time to change
your mind, ticket, journey,
point of departure,
Estimated Time of Arrival
and know that she will lend you wings
for those golden slippers, milk and honey,.
bread, roses and a brand new map.

RICHARD TILLINGHAST

Firstness

Early pleasures please best, some old voice whispers:
Cosy holdings, the heart's iambic thud
And sly wanderings – lip-touchings, long summers,
The rain's pourings and pipings heard from bed,
Earth-smell of old houses, airy ceilings,
A boy's brainy and indolent imaginings.

Twenty summers gone then that boy is gone,
Speeding down beach roads in a friend's MG.
Love, or the limey buzz of a g n' t –
Or better, both – and the watery hunter's moon,
Accelerate the engines of the night,
And set a long chase afoot.

Today, twenty years older than that even,
I breathe quietness and fresh-laundered linen,
Kneeling, seeing with eyes opened white brick,
Smelling Sunday, mumbling beside my son those words
About a lost sheep, and someone's having erred.
Thank God for instinct, and beginner's luck.

CAROLE SATYAMURTI

Tuesday at the Office

A human fly has climbed the pylon.
Stripped, but for shoes,
('I hope he gets sunburn,' Sandra says)
he's black against postcard blue.
We can't hear him, only see mimed anger
as he shouts down to firemen
perched on puny ladders, offering food.
('Waste of public money,' Sandra says.)

It's like golf on TV.
We chat, type, photo-copy,
looking up between jobs
at our man, monkeying about.
If he's going to jump, we want to see,
be made solemn, half hoping
it'll make sense of something.
('I know it's a cry for help, but,' Sandra says.)

At some point, he's gone.
That night, we watch Thames News
to prove it happened, and we were there.
But there's no mention,
only traffic and a murder,
so he must have climbed quietly
back into his ordinary life.
('I knew he'd let us down,' Sandra says.)

Note
Commissioned by the Scunthorpe Musical Festival Society.

You Make Your Bed

You make your bed, precisely not to lie on it
but to confine the disorder of the night
in mitred corners, unruffled surfaces.

Morning's already clamouring in your head.
This is a stand against incompetence
– at least one perfectly accomplished act.

All day it's what you've put behind you,
a baby place that, with the dark, draws you
down, and back; an enticing book

whose soft covers you open, slipping into
those quotidian rehearsals, love
and sleep. And dream irresponsibly

until the bell clangs for the next round.
Loth to climb out, you know you should be glad
you can. You make your bed precisely . . .

ROBERT COLE

Mending

In memory of my Father

He picked the rusty thread out with tweezers,
examined it like a fly in honey.
The escapement unspooled, glinted
under his reading-lamp lashed to the socket.

His jeweller's eye-piece flashed
a bead drawn down, dewdrops of light
moistened his forehead, sweating dynamite
over the time-piece.

His crystal-set gleamed, tuned into
Vaughan Williams, wavering notes a jangle
of Arabic bone-flutes he explained away
as sun-spots. The dial pitted with fox-marks.

He'd had his watch in the desert. Gun-metal
strap, face pranged. Flesh closed over
where a bullet scorched a starburst on his wrist.
He steadied a screwdriver.

Cogs whirled from their housing.
He placed them in a pool of oil on a tin tray,
released the new spring, a golden hair
to be wound in a sweet-heart's locket.

RUTH FAINLIGHT

Flowing Stream

Shadows of leaves
on the pavement I'm laying
with stones from the garrigue
are drifting across it
like clear water in a shallow stream.

Shadows of chestnut
acacia and elder leaves
ripple like water in sunlight
over smooth pale stones
which might be a stream bed.

The movement of shadows
silhouettes of leaves
speckle the cobbles, the wave-worn
limestone slabs of unclassifiable
lichen-splotched shapes

and alter the pattern
by glittering refraction
as the water eddies
around fallen twigs and pebbles
on the sandy stream bed, on the paving

until I don't know
whether shadows or reflections
wind or stones or leaves
are transparent water
in a flowing stream.

Romance

Every time I fold the laundry
I remember when she told me how
it took an hour to put his clothes away,
and that meant every day.

Eyes flashing, she made the list
of her duties into a metaphor.
She looked like a Minoan goddess, or Yeats'
princess bedded on straw.

She seemed to gloat on the servitude,
as if it were the fuel and source
of her obsession, and each passionate protest
a further confirmation.

My spirit shrivelled, like fingers
from harsh soap and cold water,
to see it through her eyes. She frightened me,
yet I never doubted.

Fairy-tales are very specific,
almost domestic – tasks to be done,
problems to solve. They tell about bewitched
princesses, toad princes,

and the force that holds them spell-bound.
Smoothing his shirts, she dreamed
of transformation and reward, and being
happy ever after.

I'd gone down that road before,
and knew its forks and sudden twists
where one false step has mortal consequence.
But I was luckier.

RICHARD KELL

The Divorcee and the Widower

Cool, guarded, she weighs him up. At least
that's what she thinks she's doing, but in fact
he's in the make-up chair: a standard Beast
is forming at her touch – the eyebrows blacked
and spread like raven wings, a shadowed stare
recalling one that drove her to despair.

Now every word he offers will attest
his patriarchal guilt. Her programmed brain
is satisfied that he's 'like all the rest' –
male-chauvinistic, lustful, selfish, vain.
He's trapped: for how would silence, or a smile,
go down in her interrogation file?

Though monster, he supports all human rights,
and therefore women's – can even understand
why, made for popes and merchants, kings and knights,
expressions long in service are unmanned.
No wonder there's a boom in lesbian love
and heteromanticism gets the shove.

The trouble is – well, isms. Where they rise,
new dogmas and constraints replace the old.
He hints at such misgivings, but her eyes
assure him that the effort leaves her cold.
Then, in a pause, her image disappears
and memory floats him back across the years.

He sees a devil-husband, one who dips
small bottoms and vaginas in the suds,
with creamy spoonfuls coaxes blobby lips,
shakes baby-talc on penises like buds;
who digs, repairs, paints walls and windowsills,
holds down a stressful job to meet the bills.

What if he told her that? Would she respond –
cancel the pointed ears, the fangs, the tail,
and, newly gentle, recognize a bond
between the female psyche and the male? –
or, unforgiving, grimly partisan,
despise him to the end for being a man?

MICHEAL O'SIADHAIL

Embrace

The evening guests arrive all flowers and wine
and loud hellos at the gate. *Come on, come in.*
Good to see you! Just a bottle for the kitchen.
I kiss the women's cheeks; between us men
a handshake, our gesture and show of strength,
this double signal – hands-on and armslength.

I want to fling my limbs open and embrace.
A clumsy left hand glances a shoulder blade
and I know at once he's feeling some hand laid
to measure a deal's anxiety, nervous giveaways.
A hug is a dagger too close, a dealer's grope.
Something tightens at my touch and buttons up.

I'll take your coat. Flowers. You shouldn't have!
We shy from such receiving, a chink in the male
like a sideways revelation and a hurried withdrawal
or some blurted late-night confidence brushed off
in a morning-after silence or averted look.
Was I bad? I remembered nothing when I woke.

What have we done to ourselves? Years of tautness,
a gaucheness hiding its face behind our ritual,
a coil and wriggle in ourselves we want to veil.
Look! how those women caress and touch with ease.
Sisters, sisters, it's us you're trying to free;
more than your scorn, our dealer's grope needs pity.

And weren't you women once those mothers drying
up our tears? A face shown and withdrawn.
Slugs and snails and puppy dogs. *Stand like a man.*
Tell me, did you ever see your father crying?
A coin's faces, each a keeper for the other.
Woman and man, somehow we're in this together.

SEAMUS HEANEY

An Architect

Something always at stake or being staked.
He fasted on the doorstep of his gift,
Exacting more, minding the far boulder

And raked gravel of zen. But no slouch either
When it came to the whiskey, whether to
Lash into it or just to lash it out.

Courtly, rapt, also slightly astonishing –
Like the afternoon he stepped out of his clothes
And waded in step in his pelt along the beach.

Exit now, in his tweeds, down an aisle between
Drawing boards as far as the eye can see
To where it can't until he sketches where.

FLEUR ADCOCK

Sub Sepibus

(*'Many of this parish in the years ensuing were marryed clandestinely, i.e.* sub sepibus, *and were excommunicated for their labour.'* – Note after entries for 1667 in Parish Register for Syston, Leicestershire)

Under a hedge was good enough for us,
my Tommy Toon and me –
under the blackthorn, under the may,
under the stars at the end of the day,
under his cloak I lay,
under the shining changes of the moon;
under Tom Toon.

No banns or prayer-book for the likes of us,
my Tommy Toon and me.
Tom worked hard at his frame all day,
but summer nights he'd come out to play,
in the hedge or the hay,
and ply his shuttle to a different tune –
my merry Tom Toon.

The vicar excommunicated us,
my Tommy Toon and me.
We weren't the only ones to stray –
there are plenty who lay down where we lay,
and have babes on the way.
I'll see my tickling bellyful quite soon:
another Tom Toon.

Nellie

In memory of Nellie Eggington, 1894–1913

Just because it was so long ago
doesn't mean it ceases to be sad.
Nellie on the sea-front at Torquay
watching the fishing-boats ('Dear Sis and Bro,
I am feeling very much better') had
six months left to die of her TB.

She and Marion caught it at the mill
from a girl who coughed and coughed across her loom.
Their father caught it; he and Marion died;
the others quaked and murmured; James fell ill.
So here was Nellie, with her rented room,
carefully walking down to watch the tide.

When she'd first been diagnosed, she'd said
'Please, could Eva nurse me, later on,
when it's time, that is . . . if I get worse?'
Eva swallowed hard and shook her head
(and grieved for fifty years): she had her son
to consider. So their mother went as nurse.

Nellie took her parrot to Torquay –
her pet (as she herself had been a pet,
Eva's and her father's); she could teach
words to it in the evenings after tea,
talk to it when the weather was too wet
or she too frail for sitting on the beach.

Back in Manchester they had to wait,
looking out for letters every day,
or postcards for 'Dear Sis'. The winter passed.
Eva and Sam made plans to emigrate.
(Not yet, though. Later.) April came, and May –
bringing something from Torquay at last:

news. It was Tom's Alice who glanced out,
and called to Eva; Eva called to Sam:
'Look! Here's Mother walking up the road
with Nellie's parrot in its cage.' No doubt
now of what had happened. On she came,
steadily carrying her sharp-clawed load.

HELEN DUNMORE

In the Desert Knowing Nothing

Here I am in the desert knowing nothing,
here I am knowing nothing
in the desert of knowing nothing,
here I am in this wide
desert long after midnight

here I am knowing nothing
hearing the noise of the rain
and the melt of fat in the pan

here is our man on the phone knowing something
and here's our man fresh from the briefing
in combat jeans and a clip microphone
testing for sound,
catching the desert rain, knowing something,

here's the general who's good with his men
storming the camera, knowing something
in the pit of his Americanness
here's the general taut in his battledress
and knowing something

Here's the boy washing his kit in a tarpaulin
on a front-line he knows from his GCSE
coursework on Wilfrid Owen
and knowing something

here is the plane banking,
the *go go go* of adrenalin
the child melting
and here's the grass that grows overnight
from the desert rain, feeling for him
and knowing everything

and here I am knowing nothing
in the desert of knowing nothing
dry from not speaking.

Poem for a Satellite

The snow puts its hands over our eyes –
what does it hide
from us, what does it hide
from a winking satellite
slung in its string bag
across the path of sunlight and moonlight?

An orange in a net of stars –
spiked with electronics
sly as a grandma pretending
she can't find us
when it's easy-peasy.
I'm coming! Coo-eee!

Stop. Listen. They're looking
to the stars for intelligence.
Let it snow more
like a hand wiping away the lines
of sickness, the bird-black
lines of communication.

CAROL RUMENS

A Dialogue of Perestroishiks

Good riddance to that old eyesore, the Engine of Justice
Ah, but the Engine of Justice was theoretically beautiful
Ah, but the Engine of Justice was all bloody theory
Ah, but it went, the good old Engine of Justice
Ah, but it never ran on time, the Engine of Justice
Ah, but the Engine of Justice was greased lightning in its heyday,
    and it could sing 'How Great is Our Motherland' in four parts
Ah, but the Engine of Justice was ecologically unsound, and
                    it stank to high heaven
Ah, but everyone on board the Engine of Justice had a job
Ah, but the Engine of Justice was a dictatorship
Ah, but the Engine of Justice was a dictatorship of the
                    proletariat
Ah, but the Engine of Justice gave fat hand-outs to the bosses
Ah, but the Engine of Justice put potatoes in all the children
Ah, but the Engine of Justice knew nothing about female
                    orgasm
Ah, but what d'you expect of an Engine of Justice?
Ah, but did you hear the one about the Engine of Justice?
Ah, but there have been some grand stories about the Engine
                    of Justice
Ah, but the Engine of Justice was a fabulous all-time con
Ah, but the Engine of Justice only needed a new oil-can
Ah, but the Engine of Justice only needed a new definition
                    of Justice
Ah, but who will build us a better Engine of Justice?
Ah, but each man should aim to be his own Engine of Justice,
              and each woman too, of course
Ah, but the Engine of Justice was for everyone
Ah, but was everyone for the Engine of Justice?
Ah, but anyway, I had a soft spot for the dear old Engine of
                    Justice

Ah, but the dear old Engine of Justice eliminated people for
                                                    having soft spots
Ah, but, excuse me, what have you got in your hand if it
                isn't the plans for a new Engine of Justice?
Ah, but we're not calling it the Engine of Justice
Ah, but it looks very similar to
Ah, but it's not, so shut up
Ah, but
Ah but ah but?
Ah
Ah!

CAROL ANN DUFFY

Moments of Grace

I dream through a wordless, familiar place.
The small boat of the day sails into morning,
past the postman with his modest haul, the full trees
which sound like the sea, leaving my hands free
to remember. Moments of grace. *Like this.*

Shaken by first love and kissing a wall. *Of course.*
The dried ink on the palms then ran suddenly wet,
a glistening blue name in each fist. I sit now
in a kind of sly trance, hoping I will not feel me
breathing too close across time. A face to the name. *Gone.*

The chimes of mothers calling in children
at dusk. *Yes.* It seems we live in those staggering years
only to haunt them; the vanishing scents
and colours of infinite hours like a melting balloon
in earlier hands. The boredom since.

Memory's caged bird won't fly. These days
we are adjectives, nouns. In moments of grace
we were verbs, the secret of poems, talented.
A thin skin lies on the language. We stare
deep in the eyes of strangers, look for the doing words.

Now I smell you peeling an orange in the other room.
Now I take off my watch, let a minute unravel
in my hands, listen and look as I do so,
and mild loss opens my lips like No.
Passing, you kiss the back of my neck. A blessing.

Stafford Afternoons

Only there, the afternoons could suddenly pause
and when I looked up from lacing my shoe
a long road held no one, the gardens were empty,
an ice-cream van chimed and dwindled away.

On the motorway bridge, I waved at windscreens,
oddly hurt by the blurred waves back, the speed.
So I let a horse in the noisy field sponge at my palm
and invented, in colour, a vivid lie for us both.

In a cul-de-sac, a strange boy threw a stone.
I crawled through a hedge into long grass
at the edge of a small wood, lonely and thrilled.
The green silence gulped once and swallowed me whole.

I knew it was dangerous. The way the trees
drew sly faces from light and shade, the wood
let out its sticky breath on the back of my neck,
and flowering nettles gathered spit in their throats.

Too late. *Touch*, said the long-haired man
who stood, legs apart, by a silver birch
with a living, purple root in his hand. The sight
made sound rush back, birds, a distant lawnmower,

his hoarse, frightful endearments as I backed away
then ran all the way home; into a game
where children scattered and shrieked
and Time fell from the sky like a red ball.

PHILIP GROSS

Time Out

There's a curt breeze up.
A grainy whiteness
far out. One gull looking for its shadow

on a mile of sand. Light
like a locked-up supermarket.
And you, how strange, it's you.

White wrought-iron chairs
are leaning, elbows on their tables.
All the parasols are down

but one. It hackles and slaps
above you. You're taking your ease
deep out of season

in that bleached-out frock, arms bare,
leaning back like a lady of leisure.
You ought to be chilled to the bone.

To a life
spent doling cups of kindness!
Now you drink, disgracefully, alone

taking clear water straight
on the rocks, strong as gin.
The glass sweats with the cold.

The wind is impatient,
it wants to sweep under our feet.
You won't be hurried now.

A newspaper peels itself
page by page, and every one
is white. What news?

There's silence in it.

RODNEY PYBUS

Black Swan

Black bird, white shadow. The snowy banks
of the river are closing each hour
on the channel of free water.

Two swans, a stranger and trailing
mute familiar, head upstream before
the next blizzard drives.

You show us the antipodes
of our better selves – cinder beauty
with crushed-strawberry beak

ringed once as if by rime,
your red-rimmed black eye glinting
warm and furious at the crime

of my being here in the snow, too close.
I can see how one of us couldn't bear you
elsewhere, took the clippers to your wings.

Now in February, with no sign of thaw
in this hardening world, I fear
you'll die of our black hearts.

JOHN SEWELL

From the Book of a Hundred Facts

You were on your back, eyes closed, arms out, your clothes
beside you. There was the sound of a plane
in the distance, voices from across the lake.
It was the time when water crowfoot slows
the current – daisy beds buoyed high into the light,
so the young coot in grey velvet can snow-step
bank to bank, while a bullock meanders
through an uncut field that could keep him sweet
through the longest winter. In the grass – fragments
of speckled shell, a downy scattering of feathers
broadcast through the stitchwort, the white and red
campion. I might have pulled you from the river
you lay so still, were you not so warm
to my finger, or smiling quite so much.

JOHN LUCAS

Really the Blues

Time was at the after-school Rhythm Club
a ten-play needle dipped in *Cognac Blues*
scored grooves along my heart. Now, when I taste
brandy it's a white-hot glissade of notes
sheering across my tongue to star my eyes:
love found me out in a bare-bulb classroom.

Soon, I had it set up in my bedroom.
All the cats came to wail at the HOT CLUB
of Lilac Crescent, Staines. I'd shade my eyes
and when ol' George wailed *Burgúndy Street Blues*
I stepped alongside, in my hatband notes
for bootleg red-eye with a bite to taste.

'No one with any semblance of good taste,'
my mother said, 'would give such foul noise house room,'
and now Next-Door was leaving nasty notes,
and why could I not join a proper club!
I told her then, 'What's proper is the Blues:
open your ears, the Blues will open your eyes.'

I sent for *Doctor Jazz* and closed my eyes.
What was it with red peppers that their taste
raised such a storm? And what of the cloudy blues
of Beryl's eyes? 'Come on up to my room
after you've called Time at the Legion Club'
I'd scrawled in the most recent of my notes.

Back came a note to end all other notes.
I read it screwing up my smoke-dazed eyes:
'What, just so I can get put in the Club?
No thanks. And trad jazz, dad, is last year's taste.
Blueberry Hill is where it's at, not *Blue Room*
or *Basin Street*.' That really gave me the blues.

Time for the Empress's *Down-Hearted Blues*.
I took the obbligato, bent the notes,
and blew them to all corners of the room.
The audience was gate-mouthed, tear-washed eyes
confessed that here at last was the true taste
of Loveless Love. So, welcome to the club.

And that's the Blues for you. Back of the eyes
notes splintered as I savoured the dark taste
a room has when it turns Lonely-Hearts Club.

Three Women that Live in Art
A Triptych

Gislebert's 'Eve', in Autun, Burgundy

Snake is implicit in the Tree
   whose ringstraked branches curve like ropes
to proffer Eve ripe apples, free.

Her seed lies hidden, like the pips
   in clustered grapes on coiling vines
that spread their fan to veil her hips.

Snake glides between her chiselled lines –
   combed parallel – of wavy hair,
and undulates, as Eve reclines,

in limbs that swim for Time's fresh air
   out of Eternity's arrest.
She cannot live as pure Idea.

I see a schoolgirl's nubile breast
   and greedy profile; know her eye
lacks innocence, is filled with lust

to pierce the skin of latency.

Mother with Two Children by Egon Schiele

My fruit devours me, drinks me,
lives by my depletion;
these are my rosy apples,
my painted clowns, my children
that brighten as I fade.

They rise out of my ashes
in multi-coloured plumage –
striped coats and vivid sashes
like pretty patchwork gypsies –
the dolls my body made

that sit on both my hands.
I am not free, not free
but bound and mute. Love thinks me
fulfilled: a laden tree.

A Duccio Madonna and Child

for Pamela Izzard, and in memory of Polly

Mourning mother of a mortal god,
   the mannikin you weep for dries your tears
but still you weep, till your blue cloak and hood
   are dark as midnight with clairvoyant fears.
You have condemned an innocent to die.
   The mandatory price for drawing breath
is death by want, disease, time's atrophy
   or crucifixion; and you know this truth
too well, for – changing like Madonna Moon –
   you will yourself betray and undermine
and execute, then – laying out your son –
   will drain his blood and strip his skeleton.
Therefore you grieve, while offering with love
Earth's playground crazed with pathways to the grave.

VICKI FEAVER

Starry Night

A pious town, with a tall steeple
that points to heaven.
Behind lit windows people are laying
bread and soup on the tables
and praying: *Dieu soit béni!*

It's a wild night: the stars
twirling in their sockets;
cypresses twisting up
out of the red clay
like flames.

The doctor's had two calls:
a child struggling to be born –
forcing a passage through rings
of rigid muscle; and a man
with a cancer of the larynx

who's breathing
as if he were running.
It's his friend the schoolmaster.
They spent evenings smoking
cherry tobacco and playing chess.

When the doctor's wife ran off
with a violinist, he advised:
'She'll come back to you
if you can leave her alone' –
and was proved right.

The girl in childbirth
is the dressmaker's daughter:
seventeen years ago he held her
by the heels, smacked
the first cry out of her throat.

He finishes his soup:
a thick broth of mutton
and barley and carrots.
He's a brave man
who doesn't flinch

from using saw or scalpel
on patients tied
to his surgery chair.
But there's nothing he can do
to help his old friend out,

or ease the child in,
that won't risk their souls
swirling up in the wind's currents
and sweeping without meeting
past an orange moon.

DANNIE ABSE

The Excavation

Absurd those tall stories of tall heroes.
Mine, too. Sixty ells, they said, between
my shoulders! Happy legends of my strength!
Hippy myths of my hair! How I lifted up
a mountain here, a mountain there. Dig, dig:
so little recorded, so many exaggerations.

Three hundred foxes, they said, remember?
Nine, only nine. With a jawbone of an ass,
they said, I topped a thousand men. Dig, dig
for their gritty skulls. I unthatched a mere ten.
Let others boast that I was 'magic',
the rainbow spirit of the Lord about me.

But absent, He, when the whips cracked and I
was led, eyeless, into Dagon's Temple,
heard the hooting crazies on the roof. So many,
the junk Temple collapsed thunderously.
Joke! They thought *I'd* brought the House down –
me, clapped-out circus act, defunct Strong Man.

I was screaming, believe me, I was lost.
Betrayed, betrayed, and so little recorded:
the brevities of a Hebrew scribe only;
a fable for a Milton to embroider;
a picture for a Rubens to paint;
music for the soul of a Saint-Saëns.

Dig, dig, though you will not find Dagon's
stone fish-tail nor the scissors of the sung star
of the Philistines. Who knows the path of that whore
after the Temple, unglued, crashed and crushed?
Did she return to Sorek or raise once more
her aprons in the brothels of Philistia?

Dig, dig. I hear your questing spades muffled,
south of Gaza. Useless. The shifting sands
have buried deeper the graves of all.
Only the wilderness remains, silence
and a jawbone. And marvellous ghosts
people a yellow page of Judges.

On the Evening Road

A disgrace a man of my age
to have come this far and not to know;
the fields inert with ignorant mist,
the road between, lost, unsignposted.

I may as well sing a little
since no one's around to hear me,
'The Song of Omega' my father sang
though the words I've mostly forgotten.

I may as well dance a bit, too,
since no one's around to scold me:
'Disgrace, a man of his age singing
drunkenly – not knowing where he is.'

Now the Caladrius bird lands
as it must, on the road ahead of me
and drops its dung. Turn towards me, bird,
O turn, turn, with your yellow beak.

Note
*Caladrius bird: A white, prophetic bird of medieval legend,
supposed to visit the sick. If it looked at the patient he/she
would recover; if it looked away, the patient would die.*